I CAN PRAY THE ROSARY!

...and remember Jesus and Mary

Mary Terese Donze, A.S.C.

LIGUORI
PUBLICATIONS

One Liguori Drive
Liguori, MO 63057-9999
(314) 464-2500

Imprimi Potest:
James Shea, C.SS.R.
Provincial, St. Louis Province
The Redemptorists

Imprimatur:
Monsignor Maurice F. Byrne
Vice Chancellor, Archdiocese of St. Louis

ISBN 0-89243-335-3

Cover art by Pam Hummelsheim
Interior art by Mary Terese Donze, A.S.C.

CONTENTS

INTRODUCTION

Hi....

Do you ever think about things that happened to you or to your family? When you do think about these things, it's like having a TV right in your head. You can almost see it happen all over again. If you are remembering fun at the pool, you can see the water and hear your friends laughing and feel how cool and wet the water was. If you are thinking about something that was not a fun time, like the time your dog ran away and you were worried, you can see that in your mind too. And you can remember how sad you were.

When we pray the rosary, we remember some happy and some sad things that we know about Jesus and Mary, and we let our hearts feel happy or sad with them.

This booklet will show you how to pray the rosary, and the pictures will help you think of Jesus and Mary while you pray. Soon you will come to know and love Jesus and Mary more and more. This will make you happy now and get your heart ready to see Jesus and Mary face to face in heaven some day.

THE JOYFUL MYSTERIES

1. The Annunciation

God sent an angel to Mary to ask her if she would be the mother of Jesus. Mary thought about it for a while in her heart. It would be wonderful, but it would not be easy. Jesus was going to have to suffer. But because she loved God very much, Mary said "Yes."

Today God does not send angels with messages. God could, of course. But most of the time God uses our parents or our teachers or the priests at church to tell us what to do. And sometimes God talks to us right in our hearts.

When we hear God talking to us, do we listen? Do we think about it and pray about it and then say, "All right. I'll do it"?

Mary, help me to love God more so that I will always say "Yes" when God wants me to do something — even if it is hard.

2. The Visitation

The angel told Mary that her cousin Elizabeth was also going to have a baby. Babies are very nice. But they make extra work, so Mary hurried to Elizabeth's house to help.

Elizabeth was happy that the mother of Jesus came to see her. Elizabeth's joy made Mary even happier about Jesus. Mary made up a lovely song and sang it to thank God for being so kind to her and to all of us — because Jesus would be for all of us, you know, not just for Mary.

Do we help others when they have extra work? Do we do it cheerfully, with a song on our lips or in our hearts? If we do, we will be like Mary. We will be bringing Jesus into the lives of others.

Mary, let me praise God with you for Jesus. Then get me used to looking around to see if I can help somebody for Jesus' sake.

11

3. The Birth of Jesus at Bethlehem

If Jesus had been born at home, Mary would have had plenty of blankets, and Joseph would have kept the house warm. But God let Jesus be born poor and in a stable so no one would ever feel afraid to come to him. Nobody is afraid to come to a poor little baby lying in a nest of dry grass in a barn. But even though he looked little and helpless, Jesus was still the great and wonderful God.

God is in each of us. Sometimes we find it hard to believe that God is in people we don't like. It's like looking at Jesus on the hay and saying, "That can't be God. God would be dressed a lot nicer and live in a big house."

Maybe we need to think about the people we don't like or don't want to bother about and ask God to make us remember that what we do to them we are doing to God in them.

Mary, if God loves *me* no matter what, help me to love other people — no matter what.

4. The Presentation of the Child Jesus in the Temple

Mary and Joseph took the infant Jesus to the big church in Jerusalem to make an offering of him to God. A man named Simeon lived in Jerusalem. God had told Simeon that he would not die until he had seen Jesus, the Savior. That day God put it into Simeon's mind to go to the church. And there he saw Jesus. If he hadn't gone, he would have missed him.

God has many graces ready for each of us. If we pray and try to listen to what God wants us to do, God will see that we get all these graces. If we don't pray or try to listen, we won't be around when God is handing out the graces for us — it's something like that. We need to have our hearts open and ready so God can find a place in us to leave the graces that are meant for us.

Mary, make my heart ready for the graces God wants to give me.

5. The Finding of the Child Jesus in the Temple

Jesus grew up in Nazareth and went to the church in town. When he was twelve, Joseph and Mary took him to the big church in Jerusalem again. It took a few days to get there. When they were ready to come home, Jesus was nowhere around. After looking a long time, Mary and Joseph found him in the big church, preaching to some grownups about God. He was just a boy, but the grownups listened.

When we love people, we like to talk about them. If we never talk about God, maybe it is because we don't love God as much as we might. Or maybe we feel shy about talking about God. But once we speak about God in a truly honest way, we may be surprised at how many people, even grownups, will be glad to listen and will begin to feel it is all right to talk about God.

Mary, help me love Jesus so much that I often find myself talking about him to other people.

THE SORROWFUL MYSTERIES

1. The Agony of Jesus in the Garden

The night before Jesus died he went out into a garden to pray. He took Peter, James, and John with him. They were three of his apostles. It was lovely out under the stars. But Jesus was sad. He knew he was going to be killed the next day, and his friends didn't understand. They slept while Jesus prayed. He felt very lonely, so lonely his heart felt broken. But he kept on praying, and his heavenly Father sent an angel to give him courage to say "Yes" to what was going to happen.

Sometimes we feel lonely. It seems as if nobody likes us or cares about us, or it seems like everything we do goes wrong. Jesus knows the feeling. He wants us to pray as he did. We won't see an angel come to help us, but God will put strength and courage in our hearts to say "Yes" to what he wants. With God helping, nothing will be too hard for us. But we must pray!

Mary, help me understand that when things go wrong and I pray, I get a share of God's great strength.

2. The Scourging at the Pillar

The Roman Governor Pontius Pilate ordered the soldiers to whip Jesus — and not just a few swats. They hit him many times with heavy ropes. They could hit hard because they were strong men. Jesus was God. He could have stopped them, but he suffered all this to make up for our sins.

Almost nobody can understand how bad sin really is. It is so terrible that Jesus put up with all this pain. From now on, before we start to do something bad, let us stop and think of Jesus and say, "No, I won't do this. It is a sin. Jesus died so I could be good and someday be with him in heaven. The devil wants me to be bad, but I won't."

Mary, when the thought comes to me to do something bad, help me remember how much Jesus suffered for me.

23

3. The Crowning With Thorns

After the soldiers had whipped Jesus, they made a crown out of some twigs from a thornbush. They put it on Jesus' head to make fun of him, pretending they thought he was a king. Jesus didn't fight them off. He knew they didn't really know him or they wouldn't do what they were doing. In his heart he prayed for them.

It is not easy to pray for people who hurt us. Most of us like to fight back and get even. And sometimes we do that. But Jesus tells us that we will "get even" in a much better way if we pray for these people who hurt us because it will help them get over being bad. Then all of us will be getting even with the devil, who wants us to do these wrong things. It is all right to get even with him.

Mary, I find it hard to be nice to people who hurt me. Help me be kind to them anyway for Jesus' sake.

25

4. Jesus Carries His Cross

The people who said Jesus had to die made him carry a cross. They were going to nail him to it. It was a heavy piece of wood. It had to be heavy or it would have bent when they nailed Jesus to it. Jesus was so tired and hurting that he fell a few times while he carried the cross. But he always got up and went on.

A very holy man called Saint Paul once said that trying to be good is like running a race. Sometimes in a race, people stumble and fall. That is what happens to us too. It is not always easy to be good. Once in a while we do wrong things, we commit sins. That is like falling down. What we need to remember is to get up and try again like Jesus did when he fell down. Jesus will help us.

Mary, when I fall into sin, pray for me to get up and start over again, remembering that Jesus will always give me the courage I need.

5. The Crucifixion and Death of Our Lord

They nailed Jesus to the cross. They used spikes because little nails would not hold. For three hours — that's like from lunchtime to when school is out — Jesus hung on the cross. It was terrible. But he wasn't thinking of himself. He forgave the people who did this to him. Then he turned to his mother standing near the cross and told her to be a kind mother to all of us. Afterward he said "Yes" to God and died.

If we let Jesus fill our hearts with faith, we will know that God always allows only what is best to happen in our lives. Sometimes it doesn't seem that way. It is at those times, when it is hard to say "Yes" to God, that we need to believe more than ever that God truly loves us and that someday he will make everything, *everything,* right in heaven.

Mary, help me trust in God and learn to wait.

29

THE GLORIOUS MYSTERIES

1. The Resurrection

On the third day after Jesus died on the cross, an angel came from heaven and rolled back the stone from the tomb where they had laid him. Jesus stepped out alive, happy, his body all healed and beautiful. Birds sang, the flowers bloomed, and everyone who heard about Jesus being alive again rushed about and told everyone else. It was a glorious Easter Sunday!

Death was not the end for Jesus. It was really the beginning of another wonderful kind of life. It will be that way for us too. Someday we will come alive again after we die, too, if we have tried to say "Yes" to what God wants us to do. We will be with all our friends, happy and healthy and full of joy. Our bodies will be changed so they can't die anymore. It will be our own Easter Sunday. It will be Jesus' special gift to us.

Mary, I rejoice with you that Jesus came back to life. Help me remember that someday I will have this new life too.

33

2. The Ascension

Jesus stayed with his apostles and friends for forty happy days after he rose from the dead. Then one day he walked out into a field with them and said good-bye and went to heaven. He told them not to be sad. He said they should go back to the town and be his Church, and he would still be with them. They wouldn't see him with their eyes, but he would be near them until the end of the world.

Jesus is with us in the Mass and holy Communion. But he is with the pope and the bishops in a special way so they can watch over his Church and teach us what we should know about God and about how to get to heaven.

We should thank God for giving us the Church and pray often for the pope and the bishops.

Mary, even when I grow up and get out of school, help me keep on learning more about what God wants me to know about his Church.

3. The Coming of the Holy Spirit

When Jesus' apostles and friends came back to the city after Jesus went to heaven, they stayed in the house most of the time. They were afraid that the people who killed Jesus might kill them too. But after nine days Jesus sent them the Holy Spirit. This Holy Spirit of God took away their fear and filled them with courage and joy. They unlocked the doors and went out and preached loudly and everywhere about Jesus.

Sometimes we feel shy about being Catholics. We know people won't kill us for it, but we think they will make fun of us. We need to ask the Holy Spirit to fill us with courage so we will not be afraid to let people know we are Catholic but will rejoice in our faith and want to share our good fortune with others. We will want to spread the Good News of Jesus.

Mary, I wish I knew more about the power and sweetness of the great Holy Spirit. Ask Jesus to give me this grace.

4. The Assumption of the Blessed Virgin Mary Into Heaven

When Jesus went to heaven, he did not take his mother with him. He let her live on for a while, then die like all of us have to die. But when the time came for her to die, he came and took her to heaven. He did not take just her soul. He took her body too. There is no grave anywhere in the world with the body of the Blessed Mother in it.

When we die, Jesus takes our souls to heaven. But our bodies are put into a grave. It is the way God wants it for now. Later, God is going to make our bodies new again, and our bodies and souls will be in heaven. There will be no more crying or hurting or dying but only a time and place of wonderful joy that Jesus himself is getting ready for us. It will be like having Christmas every day, only better. How much God must love us to do all this for us!

Mary, help me to remember often about heaven and about the place that Jesus is getting ready for me. Help me to love him more.

5. The Crowning of the Blessed Mother as Queen of Heaven

No one has come back from heaven to tell us how Jesus honored his Blessed Mother when she walked into heaven. But we like to believe that he led her to a place right next to his own and praised her in front of all the angels and made her the Queen of Heaven. How proud he must have been to show off his Mother! And how happy Mary must have felt!

Mary was once just a little girl from Nazareth. Now she is Queen of Heaven. And all because she always said "Yes" to what God wanted her to do. If we learn to say "Yes" to God, we, too, will someday be honored in heaven. We will be princes and princesses in the kingdom that God is getting ready for us, not just make-believe but for real.

Mary, when I feel like I'm a nobody, let me keep in mind that no matter what anyone else thinks of me, I'm special to God. How nice!

THE PRAYERS OF THE ROSARY

Here are the prayers you need to know to say the rosary. If someone else is saying it with you, you can say the first part of each prayer and someone else can pray the part that is printed differently.

Sign of the Cross

In the name of the Father, and of the Son, and of the Holy Spirit. *Amen.*

Apostles' Creed

I believe in God, the Father almighty, creator of heaven and earth. I believe in Jesus Christ, his only Son, our Lord. He was conceived by the power of the Holy Spirit and born of the Virgin Mary. He suffered under Pontius Pilate, was crucified, died, and was buried. He descended to the dead. On the third day he rose again. He ascended into heaven, and is seated at the right hand of the Father. He will come again to judge the living and the dead. *I believe in the Holy Spirit, the holy catholic Church, the communion of saints, the forgiveness of sins, the resurrection of the body, and the life everlasting. Amen.*

Our Father (Lord's Prayer)

Our Father, who art in heaven, hallowed be thy name; thy kingdom come; thy will be done on earth as it is in heaven. *Give us this day our daily bread; and forgive us our trespasses as we forgive those who trespass against us; and lead us not into temptation, but deliver us from evil. Amen.*

Hail Mary

Hail Mary, full of grace. The Lord is with thee. Blessed art thou amongst women, and blessed is the fruit of thy womb, Jesus. *Holy Mary, Mother of God, pray for us sinners, now and at the hour of our death. Amen.*

Glory Be (Prayer of Praise)

Glory be to the Father, and to the Son, and to the Holy Spirit. *As it was in the beginning, is now, and ever shall be, world without end. Amen.*

How to Pray the Rosary

This is a picture of a rosary. Follow the steps on the next page, and you will learn how to pray the rosary.

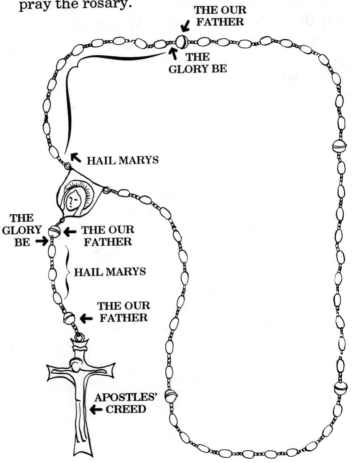

THE OUR FATHER

THE GLORY BE

HAIL MARYS

THE GLORY BE

THE OUR FATHER

HAIL MARYS

THE OUR FATHER

APOSTLES' CREED

1. Make the Sign of the Cross.
2. On the crucifix, pray the Apostles' Creed.
3. Pray the Our Father on the first large bead.
4. Pray the Hail Mary on each of the three small beads.
5. Pray the Glory Be.
6. Think about what happens in the First Mystery* and pray the Our Father.

(*If you are praying the rosary with others, you may want to announce the mystery aloud, like this: *The First Joyful Mystery, the Annunciation.* We call these prayer-thoughts mysteries because, even if we think about them a long time, we always find more to think about.)

7. Pray the Our Father on the large bead and one Hail Mary on each of the next ten small beads. Now pray the Glory Be. Do this for each of the mysteries.

More by Sister Mary Terese Donze...

In My Heart Room
16 Love Prayers for Children

This booklet helps parents encourage their children to draw closer to Christ through 16 guided meditative prayer experiences. Children learn to enter their "heart room" — where Jesus waits for them — by concentrating on everyday objects like a pencil, a penny, a flower. **$2.95**

In My Heart Room, Book Two
More Love Prayers for Children

Sister Donze brings 16 more guided "love prayers of the heart" to this follow-up collection. Children will better understand penance, the Resurrection, the Trinity, and other topics that are often difficult for them to understand as they meditate on a balloon, a garden, a leaf, and other everyday objects. **$3.95**

A Special Treat for Kids of All Ages...

365 Fun Facts for Catholic Kids
by Bernadette McCarver Snyder

Start the day the fun way — with a fun fact, a daffy definition, a saintly surprise! There's one for each day of the year in this delightful book. And each tidbit of trivia comes with a word to the wise like "be proud to be you," "stick up for what's right," and "pray EVERY day!" **$5.95**

Order from your local bookstore or write to:
Liguori Publications
Box 060, Liguori, MO 63057-9999
(Please add $1.00 for postage and handling for orders under $5.00; $1.50 for orders over $5.00.)